Special Services for Advent and Christmas

Susan Hardwick

kevin mayhew

First published in 2002 by
KEVIN MAYHEW LTD
Buxhall, Stowmarket, Suffolk IP14 3BW
Email: info@kevinmayhewltd.com

9 8 7 6 5 4 3 2 1

ISBN 1 84003 961 2
Catalogue No. 1500537

Cover design by Angela Selfe
Edited and typeset by Elisabeth Bates
Printed in Great Britain

Contents

Introduction

Can it really be time to be thinking and preparing for Advent/Christmas again, already? Surely it can't be 12 months since last time.

It is disconcerting isn't it, when you are responsible for producing original services year after year that will seek to engage the worshippers in a meaningful religious experience and give them a renewed sense of faith and wonder, how short the year can seem.

And it is similarly disconcerting how difficult it can be, when you are also busily engaged in a multitude of other important and time-consuming tasks, to find the time to think of a new slant, a different approach, from the ones used before.

To those who find a resonance in the above reflection, this book is offered as a resource.

I have selected the range of services that will, I hope, be of most use.

They are all straightforward to execute, and require only easily accessible props and music.

They are also adaptable and so can be used in their entirety or as a basic framework that can be added to or subtracted from.

The Christmas Quiz and Wordsearch can be used in a variety of ways. Here are just a few suggestions:

• to occupy children during a sermon or adult service;

• as part of a special Christmas children's section in the parish newsletter or magazine;

• a copy can be given to each child as they leave services over the Advent/Christmas season, with prizes being given to those returned with the most correct answers.

SUSAN HARDWICK

Journey to the manger (all-age)

Requirements

- Set of five Advent candles on a stand.
- Multi-directional microphone on stand, or two microphones also on stands, centre front.
- Box of delights (see Resources section).
- At one point in the service there is opportunity for some dance. This could just be rhythmic movements, swirling dancing streamers (see Resources section), or more sophisticated and choreographed, depending on the skills of those taking part.
- Approaches could be made to a local dancing school. Most are only too glad to have the opportunity to perform in different situations.
- Make it clear that parents and other relatives are most welcome to come along too. This is a good way of encouraging different people into church.
- Alternatively a more spontaneous presentation by, for example, junior members of the church should be just as welcome by the rest of the congregation and has a special charm of its own.

Note

This service tells the Christmas story through the main people involved, and so it is suggested that the various roles are taken by people who are able not only to project their voices but also the feelings behind the words.

Before the service

- As they arrive, give each child either an instrument, a windsock banner or a dancing streamer, and a head/arm/wrist/ankle-band from the Box of delights.
- Have hymns/choruses, so that there is a sense of things already happening as people enter and in which they can join. Encourage the children to use the instruments, etc., they have been given from the Box of delights.

The service

Lights: *down in main part of the church. Keep lights on at the front.* **John the Baptiser** *strides down the centre aisle and lights the* **first Advent candle**. *He goes to the microphone, centre front.*

As this is happening:

A voice (off) reading dramatically

We are going to step into our time-machine in order to be transported back in time to two thousand years ago.

The powerful Roman Empire covers much of the known world. In Rome, the mighty Emperor Tiberius has reigned for fifteen years. And Palestine, a hot, dusty and unimportant outpost of the Great Roman Empire, is ruled by Pontius Pilate and Herod.

In the Palestinian desert was living a tough young man called John. John wore simple clothes made of camel hair – *itchy*, but warm in winter and cool in summer. His food was similarly simple: a really *boring* but, it has to be admitted, healthy diet of locusts and wild honey.

Seven hundred years before this time, the prophet Isaiah (probably top guy in the league of prophets) had written:

'You will hear a voice of one that cries in the desert: "Prepare the way for the Lord! Make his paths straight and smooth! Every ditch will be filled in, every bump smoothed out, all the ruts paved over. Everyone will be there to see God's salvation."'

Chorus

The chorus of 'Make way, make way', sung several times – the number of repetitions according to the response. (329, *Hymns Old and New*)
(*Children invited to play/bang their instruments*)

John the Baptiser

I really do think Isaiah was being a bit optimistic when he said what he did; because, of course, Jesus' *birth* was, in fact, largely unnoticed by a world rushing along, eyes cast down, too busy to heed a mere chorus of angels proclaiming his birth – even though they filled the sky with their presence and their singing.

And so, just a few shepherds, some wise men from a far-off country and a few animals were the only ones who witnessed this fantastic, amazing and world-changing event.

30 years have gone by since then.

Jesus has been growing up and working in the very ordinary town of Nazareth, preparing himself for his public ministry. When God called *me* from the desert to prepare the way for Jesus – for, of course, it was he of whom Isaiah spoke all those years ago – when God called me to begin to open people's hearts and minds and to call them to repentance, I *wept* in joy and wonder.

Before I was even born, whilst I was still in my mother's womb, God lit the fire of passion for him in my heart. Since then, the flames have only burned ever brighter.

Since I came out of the desert, crowds of people have come to see me in order to hear 'the wild man of the desert' and to ask to be baptised.

But I knew many of them were probably only doing it out of curiosity, or because it was the latest craze, the popular thing to do and they didn't want to miss out – *just* in case.

I'm not known for my moderation of language, but even they were taken aback by the force of what I said!

I told them plainly that this was no soft option, something they could do today to pass the time but then, tomorrow, forget all about.

I told them they all needed to change from the *inside* out.

Also, that they needn't think that they could 'pull rank' by claiming to be the children of Abraham; that what counted was their lives and how they lived them: were they fruitful? Or was there a lot of dead wood that needed drastic pruning and burning?

I had their attention by then, I can tell you!

'What must we *do*?' they asked, as they realised this was for real.

'If you have two coats, give one away! The same with your food!' I replied.

'Taxmen: *no* more extortion! Soldiers: no intimidation. Be content with your pay!'

By now, I could hear many murmuring, 'Could this John be the Messiah we've been waiting for?'

'*No!*' I said. '*I'm* baptising you with water, in the name of One *far, far* greater than I – someone whose sandal strap I am not worthy to unfasten. But this other – Jesus is his name – *he* will baptise you with the Holy Spirit.

'He will light the fire of the Holy Spirit within you, changing you from the inside out.

'He will change and transform you, if you ask him, for he has come to change and transform the whole world.'

Then I looked up.

Jesus was standing before me!

He looked deep into my eyes. And what a gaze! I felt – no! I *knew* – he was looking deep into my very soul and could read everything that was there.

But it was such a look of *love*.

Then he spoke. 'John,' he said. 'Will you baptise *me*?'

Jesus was asking *me* to baptise *him*!

I tried to dissuade him, saying, 'It is *I* who needs baptism from *you!*'

But Jesus insisted.

After he came up out of the water, he was praying.

Then, the sky opened up and the Holy Spirit descended on him, in the form of a dove.

A voice came from heaven, saying, 'You are my Son, chosen and marked by my love, pride of my life.'

I have so often thought back to that moment. It lives with me.

I knew then that my main task was over and that, from that moment on, my ministry must decrease, as Jesus' ministry increased.

I see now that I was the bridge between the old and the new.

As the prophets foretold, I am the one who came to bear witness to the Light; paving the way for the dawning of the kingdom, which Jesus the Christ is to bring.

Who am *I*, that God should bless me so, and honour me with such a task. Such a calling.

Hymn

'I, the Lord of sea and sky' (235, *Hymns Old and New*)
(Children to be invited to accompany the hymn on their instruments.)

During the hymn: John the Baptiser exits *down side aisle.*

Mary, Mother of Jesus, enters *down the centre aisle. She lights the* **second Advent candle.**

Mary, Mother of Jesus

And who am *I*, that God should bless and honour me with such a calling, such a task?

Yet, when I look back into the history of our people, I see how God delights in using the ordinary, the everyday, to fulfil his plan.

When my cousin, Elizabeth, and I met, our unborn children within us – Elizabeth's leaping for joy at the sound of the voice of the woman who carried his Saviour – we wondered at God's graciousness towards us. That he should choose *us* – two such *ordinary* women – to fulfil his will.

We wondered, too, as all expectant mothers do, at what the future would hold for our children. But flowing beneath the excitement and apprehension was a sea of quiet faith and certainty, that God would always be closer to us than we are to ourselves.

And so it has been; for, when human beings co-operate with God, godly power is released and miracles can begin to happen.

When I said 'yes!' all those years ago, to God's messenger, I did it out of obedience and love for God. And God has honoured my obedience and love ever since.

Music

Mary exits *down side aisle, as* **dancers enter** *down centre aisle, swirling the dancing streamers as they go. One of them lights the* **third Advent candle** *at the beginning (or end) of the dance.*

As **dancers exit** *down centre aisle,* **Joseph enters** *from side aisle and lights* **fourth Advent candle**.

Joseph

When Mary said to me that an angel had visited her and told her she was to have God's Son, as you may imagine, I found it hard to believe.

Even harder to come to terms with was the fact that I thought Mary was lying to me about how she had become pregnant. I mean, *why* would God choose such a humble place and such humble people as *Nazareth* and *us*?

But then, God spoke to me in a dream and left me in no doubt whatsoever, that I should take Mary as my wife and that I had been chosen to take care of her and of her son, Jesus.

Jesus – the One who saves.

Jesus – the Son of God.

Jesus – the long-awaited Messiah.

Who am *I* – a mere carpenter – that I should be part of God's mighty plan, in this way?

Some time after this, Augustus, Emperor of Rome, who subjugates and rules over us, wished to know how many subjects he had and, thus, how much tax he could hope to collect. So, he ordered everyone to return to their hometown, in order to register for the census.

This meant everyone crisscrossing our land, from where they now lived, back to their hometown.

I had to return to Bethlehem, for I am a descendant of David of Bethlehem.

I was worried about Mary, as she was far advanced in her pregnancy. But she's a brave one! I *so* admire as well as love her.

The journey is about 70 miles and so it took us several days: Mary, on a donkey, and me walking beside. She *never* complained, though she went paler and paler as the journey progressed.

By the time we reached Bethlehem, she was exhausted and she was also getting birth pains, which were becoming stronger by the hour.

Bethlehem was *teeming* with fellow travellers. In a different situation, I would have found it all quite exciting.

But I had Mary to think of now.

All the inns were full.

We became more and more desperate each time we were turned away.

Finally, one innkeeper took pity on Mary's condition. 'I'm *sorry*, I don't have *any* rooms left. But I *do* have a stabling place, a cave, set in the hillside nearby, which you are welcome to use. It is at least warm and dry and will give you a roof over your heads.'

Of course, it was smelly and dirty, as all stables are: animal droppings on the floor and so on.

Mary's pains were coming regularly and powerfully.

We found some clean straw in a rack on the wall and I spread some out for her to lie on, then laid my cloak over her to warm her.

Then, between trying to care for her and help her, I cleaned the stable up as best I could and lined the animals' feeding trough with some more clean straw to use as a crib . . .

Joseph steps back *from the microphone and stands in an inconspicuous place, preferably in shadow. An* **innkeeper hurries down the centre aisle**. *He looks and talks agitatedly.*

Innkeeper

If *only* I'd been *told*

it was *you*.

Why,

of *course* I would

have found space

in my B and B.

Why didn't they *say*?

Why did they *let* me

turn you away?

All they wanted

was a bed,

they said.

But how was *I* supposed to know

that the weary mother-to-be

would give birth

to a child

who had been sent

to save the world

– to save *me*.

The speaker to slow down more and more as he gets nearer to the end. Finish with a note of wonder in voice.

Carol

'Silent night' (If possible, begin and end with a flute or violin solo.)

*During the carol, the **innkeeper departs** and **Joseph returns** to the microphone.*

Joseph

Eventually, there in the dimness, amongst the animal-trodden straw, Mary's baby was born.

Jesus, Saviour of the world.

Born, not in a palace, but in a hovel.

Born to bring *love* and a *new* way of living.

Mary wrapped him up – as is our custom – with long bandage strips of cloth. Then she laid him to sleep in the manger.

Joseph exits *down side aisle.*

JOURNEY TO THE MANGER

Hymn

'Be still, for the presence of the Lord' (53, *Hymns Old and New*)

Some shepherds (S1, S2, S3 and S4) enter *down the centre aisle, chatting amongst themselves.*

S1 It was an ordinary night, like any other . . .

S2 Yeah. We was sitting round the fire, chatting and telling stories, like, to keep ourselves awake . . .

S3 We'd been commenting on the stars and how bright one particular one was . . .

S4 When, all of a sudden, *the whole sky* was *aflame* with light!!! *Blazing* out, it was . . .

S3 Yeah! And *angels*. Millions of 'em. *Singing* away, so that the whole sky was *filled* with their voices.

S1 You know how timid *sheep* are. Well, the extraordinary thing was, *none* of *them* batted an eyelid, much less ran away.

S2 *Then*, one of them angels was standing *right in fron*t of us. We was *terrified*!

S1 Nah. *I* wasn't!

S2 Oh, *yes*, you *was*! Anyway, the angel said: 'Don't be frightened. I bring you good news, which will bring joy to the whole world. Go into Bethlehem . . .

S4 '. . . and there you will find a baby, lying in a manger, wrapped in swaddling clothes . . .

S3 '. . . he is the Saviour of the world.'

S1 Then all the angels poured out a hymn of praise and thanksgiving to God . . .

All 'Glory to God in the highest and peace on earth to all people.'

S3 *(shaking his head)* It was *amazing*. And the sound! So *beautiful*. Like *nothing* you've *ever* heard before. Like liquid gold . . .

S2 So, we left one of our number in charge of the sheep – he'd drawn the short straw. He weren't half cross, I can tell you, when he heard what he'd missed – and the rest of us hot-footed it into Bethlehem. Although the place was packed, we seemed to know exactly where to go. It was like we had an invisible guide directing our footsteps.

(Wonder in voices)

S4 Yeah. And there he was . . .

S3 Just as the angel had said . . .

S1 Lying in a manger . . .

S2 And we bowed down and worshipped him.

S4 Nothing will *ever* be the same again.

*One of the shepherds lights the **fifth Advent candle**.*

*Arms around each other's shoulders, **shepherds leave** down the side aisle.*

Carol

'Hark, the herald-angels sing' (vv 1 and 3) (199, *Hymns Old and New*)
Or: 'Angels from the realms of glory' (34, *Hymns Old and New*)
(Children to be invited to accompany the carol on their instruments)

(Opportunity here to put in any piece of poetry, prose, piece of music, that you wish)

Three wise men (WM1, WM2 and WM3) enter *down the centre aisle.*

WM1   There's a gentle irony that God should call us – so used to comfortable, easy living, as are we three – to endure a journey such as this. *(Chuckles)* God's sense of humour. It's *wonderful*.

WM2   *Many* months have passed since we left our families, our homes, our lands, our beloved books and instruments for tracking the movements of the firmament, to follow the bright star to its destination.

WM3   We have crossed land and water, endured the flaming rage of the desert sun and blinding sandstorms . . .

WM2   . . . Travelled through Persia to Babylon. Crossed two mighty rivers, and the Syrian wastes until, *at last*, our journey's end . . .

WM1   . . . The little town of Bethlehem. Could this *really* be the place, we wondered, where a *king* would be born? In this back-of-beyond town?

WM3   But the star that had guided us stood steady over the stable in the hillside. Our journey's end! And there in the manger, surrounded by animals, lay the reason for it all.

WM2   And we, three kings, used to *others* bowing to *us*, bowed low before the King of the world.

WM1   God's Son.

WM2   We gave him our gifts.

WM1   *Gold*, the colour of the sun. We dedicate our worldly goods to you, the Chosen One.

WM3   *Frankincense*: this holy smoke carries up our prayers.

WM2   *Myrrh* is for sorrow. Sadly, we know that one day it will come . . .

All   Most Holy Child!
Our Heavenly King!
Our gifts,
our*selves*,
to you we bring.

The wise men depart.

Heaven is here, heaven is now

Read by a child

Silent night.
The stars' pure light.
Angels winging,
their voices singing.
A babe
in the straw.
Shepherds in awe.
Wise men bow.
Heaven is here.
Heaven is now.

Prayers

Preferably written and read by a variety of ages

Blessing

May the guiding star
light your way.
May you wonder
with the shepherds
and worship with the wise men.
May you travel in faith
to your journey's end.
May the Holy Child
of Bethlehem
be born in your heart
this Christmas time.
And may the blessing of God . . .

Final carol

'Once, in Royal David's city'
(Children to be invited to accompany the carol on their instruments)
(If appropriate, the children/everyone process round the church, following the crossbearer, as the carol is sung)

Day Retreat for Advent

Length 6.5 hours

for example: 10am-4.30pm

12 noon-6.30pm

2pm-8.30pm

Try to put it on a Saturday and at a time to suit as many and as wide a variety of people as possible. If put on later in the day it enables people to do essential weekend chores, e.g. shopping, beforehand.

This Day Retreat can be extended by linking it to the Meditation Service.

Theme

Waiting in expectation and anticipation: Looking forward

Key texts

Malachi 3:1
Look, I shall send my messenger to clear a way before me.
And suddenly the Lord whom you seek
will come to his Temple;
Yes, the angel of the covenant,
for whom you long, is on his way,
says Yahweh Sabaoth.
(New Jerusalem Bible)

Luke 2:11
Today, in the town of David
a Saviour has been born to you;
he is Christ the Lord.
(New Jerusalem Bible)

Preparations

A retreat requires that the participants commit themselves to stepping aside from their normal everyday preoccupations and activities for a period of time in order to concentrate wholly on God.

There can be few events that are as likely to deepen and enrich and change people's lives so profoundly in a short period of time, as a retreat. So it is worth every minute that is invested into the planning.

Date

Fix this well in advance and advertise as widely as possible with posters, flyers and announcements.

Cost

Make it clear from the beginning how much people will have to pay, and who is eligible for reduced rates.

Venue

Decide on this as soon as possible. The style of retreat will largely be dictated by the venue.

Walk around it and be clear which space is to be used for what. With a bit of imagination, even a church hall can be turned into a very appropriate venue. Specific areas can easily be created for the different 'moods' or activities by turning a few chairs inwards to mark the boundaries.

You will need:

Worship area: Leave a space in front of the altar/table for participants to lay their offerings of pebbles/twigs/other items gathered, pictures drawn, or prose/verse written, during the day.

Resource area: Books and Bibles to aid meditation.

Activity area (if this is to be part of the retreat): e.g. paper, pencils, colouring pencils, material for collages, scissors, glue.

Points to check:

Sufficient comfortable seating: All sorts of seating can be pressed into service: e.g. garden furniture, or large cushions scattered on carpeting.

The shiver factor: Will it be warm enough?

Catering: Facilities and area/s in which to serve refreshments and food. Catering can be made much easier by asking participants to bring a packed lunch for themselves and a designated dish for a bring-and-share buffet for the other meal.

Opportunities for movement outside: Is there anywhere participants can wander outside, weather permitting.

Content of day

Be clear about what sort of retreat it is: will there be opportunities for participants to draw, paint, make collages, or will they be encouraged just to be quiet with God.

Length

Be clear about this and then stick to it.

Who is it for?

Target those whom you feel would especially benefit and encourage them to sign up.

Numbers

Decide on maximum numbers the venue can cope with and don't be tempted to go above this.

What it is

Ensure everyone understands what the day involves. Dispel any anxieties or fears and excite people with a vision of what might happen.

Silence

Is it to be partly/wholly in silence? You may need to reassure some that the silence is not something to be frightened of, that the silence can be used in a variety of ways and that, in all probability, once experienced they will not want to come out of the silence.

Worship and reflection inputs

Length

Keep within 10-15 minutes.

Suggested format

- Gentle soft meditative music for participants to come in to.
- Short Bible, or other, reading.
- Short reflection.
- Prayer.
- Meditative music, hymn or repetitive chant, e.g. 'Be still, and know that I am God'. (Explain beforehand that this will lead everyone into the silence.)

Themes and readings

Theme: If not using the suggested theme, choose an all-embracing theme to hold the whole day together and to give it a sense of unity as well as movement and progression.

Keep it simple.

The only purpose of a retreat is to provide the opportunity for the participants to step aside from their daily routine and to spend some time with God and so everything should be geared towards this.

Readings: Keep these short, especially if having more than one. Surround the key text with only as much material as you need in order to give context.

For a more detailed resource:
Retreat and quiet-day resource – Setting the scene for reflecting with God, Susan Hardwick. Published by Kevin Mayhew. (Fully photocopiable.)
A Quiet Word, Nick Fawcett. Published by Kevin Mayhew.

Day retreat programme

e.g. 9.30am-4.30pm

From 9.30am

Arrival and tea/coffee, ready for prompt start at 10am.

10-10.15am

Alpha: Welcome, explanation about the day, any questions.

10.15-10.30am

Worship and Reflection 1: 'Longing'

Bible reading: Job 23:3
If only I knew where to find him; if only I could go to his dwelling!

Hymn: 'Wait for the Lord, whose day is near' (528, *Hymns Old and New*)
        Or: 'O Love that wilt not let me go' (384, *Hymns Old and New*)

This leads into the silence.

11.30am

Coffee and biscuits.

12.30-12.45pm

Worship and Reflection 2: 'Hope'

Bible reading: Isaiah 11:1, 2
A shoot will come up from the stump of Jesse; from his roots a branch will bear fruit. The Spirit of the Lord will rest on him – the Spirit of Wisdom and Understanding, the Spirit of counsel and of power, the Spirit of knowledge and of the fear of the Lord.

Hymn: 'Spirit of the Living God' – (Repeat several times) (454, *Hymns Old and New*)

12.45pm

Lunch.

1.15pm

Into silence.

3.15pm

Tea and biscuits.

3.30-4pm

Omega: A gathering up of the day. Sharing experiences.

4-4.30pm

Holy Communion

Old Testament reading: Malachi 3:1 – 'Expected Messiah'
'See, I will send my messenger, who will prepare the way before me. Then suddenly the Lord you are seeking will come to his temple; the messenger of the covenant, whom you desire, will come,' says the Lord Almighty.

New Testament reading: Luke 2:11 – 'Promise fulfilled'
Today in the town of David a Saviour has been born to you; he is Christ the Lord. And here is a sign for you; you will find a baby wrapped in swaddling clothes and lying in a manger.

Hymns: 'How lovely on the mountain' (219, *Hymns Old and New*)
'I cannot tell how he whom angels worship' (226, *Hymns Old and New*)
'God forgave my sin in Jesus' name' (167, *Hymns Old and New*)
'I am a new creation' (221, *Hymns Old and New*)

4.30pm

Depart

Some prayers to use at the beginning and end of the day

At the beginning

Creator God,
    it is one of the mysteries and miracles
    of a retreat,
    however long or short,
    that there is time enough
    for all you would wish to work
    in us.
So help each one here today
    to remain faithful to the task;
    to be co-creators with you
    in bringing to life
    your hopes and dreams for us.
Amen.

May the Silence of God
   enfold you.
May the Love of God
   surround you.
May the Wisdom of God
   teach you.
May the Hand of God
   hold you.
May the Blessing of God
   rest upon you
   through every moment
   of this retreat.
Amen.

At the final service/time together

Lord,
   we hope we have used
   this precious time right
   and according to your wish and will.
Forgive the wasted moments.
Gather up the fragments
   that are pleasing to you:
   these are our retreat-offering.
Amen.

Thank you.
Thank you for this time.
Thank you for your care.
Thank you for your guidance.
Thank you for your faithful love.
Amen.

Generous God,
   this has been a precious,
   blessing-filled time.
Time in which to step aside
   from daily preoccupations.
Time to spend with you,
   our Creator and Redeemer,
   our Saving Grace.
Amen.

Jesus,
   walk with each one of us
   as we go from this place.
Guide our steps:
   may they be true.
May we walk only in your way.
As you have blessed us,

so may we be a blessing to others.
Make us channels of your love and peace.
We ask this in your name.
Amen.

Blessing

May the Love of God
   enfold you.
May the Strength of God
   surround you.
May the Wisdom of God
   teach you.
May the Hand of God
   hold you.
May the Blessing of God
   rest upon you
   today,
   tomorrow
   and always.
Amen.

Meditation Service for Advent

Length 75-90 minutes

The Service has four main parts. Each part contains:
- Introductory sentence: to be proclaimed.
- Reading/s
- Meditation
- Hymn
- Silence

Part Four is followed by:
- Prayers
- The Blessing
- The final hymn.

(If it is required that the length of the Service be reduced: at Part 4, have the meditation followed by silence, prayers, Blessing and the fourth hymn.)

Service: Part One

Now is the time to wake out of sleep; for our salvation is nearer than when we first believed. (Romans 13:11)

Readings

Romans 13:8-12 – 'Love, for the day is near'
Luke 21:29f – 'Heaven and earth will pass away, my words never'

Meditation: A disciple of Jesus

We'd been sitting on the Temple steps, watching the people going in and out – Jesus, the other disciples and me.

Jesus had been saying some pretty disturbing things about the Temple being destroyed and not one stone left standing; about wars and earthquakes and famines and other fearful events.

It was all pretty scary stuff, I can tell you!

Then Jesus started going on about how we could expect to be hated and persecuted and imprisoned, because we were his followers – even by friends and family! I'm sure *my* family wouldn't – would they?

However, Jesus said we mustn't worry (Huh! Sure!), because he would give us the words of wisdom we'd need in order to defend ourselves.

But then he said about the destruction of *Jerusalem* and how that would usher in a terrible time for *everyone*, with the whole world writhing in agonies.

It's at that time, Jesus told us, that the Son of Man – that's Jesus' name for himself, you know? – will come in a cloud with power and great glory.

'When these things I've described take place,' he said, *'don't* waver,' (he must be joking!) 'but stand up and lift your hands, because your redemption is drawing near.'

Then he said about the fig tree.

That's one of the *extraordinary* things about Jesus: he'll talk about storms and tempests; the sun, moon and stars melting – and then about a little fig tree, all in one breath.

I tell you, it don't half make your head spin, trying to get your brain around what he's saying, half the time.

I sense he's trying to tell us *so* much, but we're often not able to comprehend the breadth, the – the *vastness* of it all.

He must get so frustrated with us being such thickheads, but he hardly ever shows it: just smiles and thinks of another way of explaining it all, using examples taken from our own lives or life experiences.

It scares me more than anything, though, when he talks about *his* death.

I don't know what we'll do, when he's gone.

He's the world to us: teacher, friend, leader.

Tender, yet strong. So strong. Both on the *inside*, as well as on the outside. And firm as a rock.

Always laughing. Full of an inner joy that he radiates and which draws you in and warms you, through and through.

Love-light dancing in his eyes.

Love and compassion in every line of his face and body . . .

Life will have lost all its purpose if he's no longer here. He's become our reason for living . . .

Perhaps he's got it all wrong . . .

Perhaps he won't be put to death, after all . . .

Perhaps we can all grow old in each other's company, carrying on just the same as we are now: travelling around, teaching, preaching, healing, raising, spreading the Good News of God's Kingdom . . .

Perhaps the dark clouds that seem to be gathering all around us will melt away and the sun will break through again . . .

Heavenly Father, let *no* harm befall him, I *beg* of you . . .

Jesus *is* the Good News . . .

Hymn

'How lovely on the mountains are the feet of him who brings good news'. (219, *Hymns Old and New*)

Silence

Part Two

The kingdom of God is close at hand. Repent and believe the gospel.
(Micah 1:15)

Readings

Isaiah 55:6-11 – 'My thoughts are not your thoughts . . .'

Luke 4:14-21 – 'The spirit of the Lord is on me, for he has anointed me to bring the good news . . .'

John 5:30f – '. . . the Father who sent me bears witness to me himself'

Meditation: A young girl in the Synagogue

It began just as any other Sabbath Day, with all the usual religious observances since sunset the previous evening.

And yet, I had *the strangest* sense of anticipation, as though it was going to be an extra special day, in some way.

When I took my place behind the screen with the other girls and women, there seemed to be a feeling of suppressed excitement in the air.

Some of the others said they felt it too, but none of us could figure why.

We girls gave vent to our suppressed giggles, by peeking out and watching all the men file in self-importantly, and seeking a glimpse of the particular young men each of us dreams about.

I know it's Jewish custom to separate us and put us out of sight, but I can't *really* understand why we women should be treated as of no account.

Also, Jewishness is inherited through our *mothers, not* our fathers – and, in my home, like those of my friends, it is my *mother* whose word is the final one . . .

Suddenly the whole place hushed.

A young man stood in the doorway.

His presence seemed to *fill* the Synagogue.

Then he stepped into the centre and was handed the scroll from which to read the Scriptures. It is the custom to welcome and honour the stranger in this way.

Only, it *wasn't* a stranger. It was *Jesus!*

He is like a brother to me, for his youngest sister is my very best friend.

She was standing beside me, her eyes popping out of her head, as Jesus began to read from the Book of the Prophet Isaiah.

When he had finished, he rolled up the scroll, gave it back to the attendant and said: 'Today, this Scripture is fulfilled in your hearing.'

At first, the men were listening attentively as he continued to talk and they were speaking well of him.

But then, as his words became more personal and challenging, they began to fly into a rage.

It was terrifying the way the mood changed so quickly, from smiles to snarls.

Then the men rushed forward and drove Jesus out of the Synagogue and up to the top of the hills overlooking Nazareth, in order to throw him down over the steep drop and kill him!

His sisters and mother and I were screaming and tugging at them to stop. But they pushed us to one side, so that we fell sprawling in the dust.

His brothers, and the friends who had come with him, also tried desperately to intervene, but they were outnumbered.

It was *terrible*!

But then, as they stood at the brow of the hill, Jesus turned and looked at his tormentors.

They shrank back from his gaze – and Jesus walked right through the crowd.

As he passed us, kneeling still in the dust and weeping, his eyes were full of tears of sorrow and sadness, which coursed down his cheeks.

He went to his mother, gently raised her up, hugged her, touched her tear-drenched cheek tenderly with his fingers and said a few loving words.

Then he came to his sisters and me, took our hands and helped us up.

In the midst of all his own sadness and pain at his rejection by those who had been his friends and neighbours – those amongst whom he had grown up – he still found the strength and compassion to smile tenderly and reassuringly at each one of us.

'Don't be afraid,' he said. 'I have forgiven them. And so must you, so that your Father in heaven will forgive you your sins.'

Such strange words. I have pondered on them and tried to forgive, as he commanded, ever since that day.

As he went on his way I *ached* to follow him, as his male companions did.

Then, as clearly as if he had spoken the words, I knew he was telling me that I could follow him just as well, even if I stay right here in Nazareth, in my heart and in my life.

At the very moment this revelation hit me, he turned, smiled at me and nodded.

And I remembered other words from the Scriptures. From Psalm 32:

'I shall instruct you and teach you the way to go; I shall not take my eyes off you.'

Ever since that moment, I have known the truth of the matter:

That Jesus is the Christ.

The promised Messiah.

The Holy One.

The Saviour of the World.

Hymn

'God's Spirit is in my heart' (180, *Hymns Old and New*)

Silence

Part Three

When the Lord comes, he will bring to light things now hidden in darkness, and will disclose the purposes of the heart. (1 Corinthians 4:5)

Readings

Psalm 126 – The Song of the returning exiles.
Philippians 4:4-9 – 'The Lord is near. Do not be anxious about anything.'
Matthew 11:2-5 – [John asked] 'Are you the one?'

Meditation: A disciple of John

We had heard Jesus had sent his disciples off to preach, to teach and to heal, having given them authority to do all these things, in his name.

And so we weren't surprised to find only Jesus, surrounded – as usual, so I hear – by a large crowd.

As we arrived he was busily engaged in teaching the people pressing around him.

Every few minutes he would break off in order to touch hands stretched out in supplication.

Miracles of healing were happening, over and over.

And then he would resume his teaching, with no indication that the constant interruptions were a problem for him. The result was that the words and the actions seemed to flow, one into the other, each enriching the other, like a seamless whole.

He looked tired, as if the constant unremitting demand of the crowd was draining his energy. But, even so, he still never flagged or lost any of his grace and charm and tenderness towards each person.

The crowds were captivated and riveted, not only by *what* he was saying, but also by the *way* in which he taught; using stories taken straight from ordinary, everyday life and experience that everyone could relate to.

We were riveted too, and were very happy to stand on the edge of the crowd and listen and watch.

All around us, people were telling each other of others they had known who had been healed of terrible ailments such as deafness, or paralysis, or leprosy, and even raised to life by Jesus.

After some while, he turned and smiled at us. 'Welcome! John sent you, didn't he. How is my cousin?'

'Yes, Master,' our leader said. 'You are right. He *has* sent us. We are his followers.

'Herod has thrown him into prison, as you know, for daring to criticise the king's morals and behaviour – and so he could not come himself.

'He is well, though, despite his bad circumstances and experiences. His faith burns like fire within him, as ever, giving him an awesome strength in the face of his trials.'

Our leader paused, then continued, hesitantly, 'Master, John has sent us to ask: are you the One we've been expecting, or are we still waiting?'

Jesus replied, 'Go back and tell John what you hear and see:

'The blind see.

'The lame walk.

'Lepers are cleansed.

'The deaf hear.

'The dead are raised.

'The wretched of the earth learn that God is on their side.'

Our leader smiled and nodded.

'It's true, Master. Just in the short while we have been here, we have indeed heard and seen these things.'

We bowed our heads in reverence, before reluctantly taking our leave.

As we walked away, we could hear Jesus telling the crowd about John.

'What did you expect, when you went out to see him in the wild? A week-end camper? Hardly.

'What, then? A sheik in silk pyjamas? Not in the wilderness. Not by a long shot.

'What then, a prophet?

'That's right, a prophet! Probably the best prophet you'll ever hear.

'John is the prophet that Malachi announced, when he wrote: "I'm sending my prophet ahead of you, to make the road smooth for you."'

As we walked, we were all remembering John's words to us, before we set out: 'If he *is* the One, the promised Messiah, you must follow me no longer, but follow him. I am to grow less and he is to grow more.'

We had all thought our destiny was to be John's disciples.

But, isn't it just like God? '

Just when we think we're complacent and sure about the way ahead, he calls us on to something new and even more challenging than before.

I don't know about the others, for I haven't asked them yet, but I feel both excited *and* scared.

I don't know where this new direction will lead.

But one thing I *do* know: if I stay close to Jesus, I can't go far wrong.

Hymn

'Peace, perfect peace, is the gift of Christ our Lord' (414, *Hymns Old and New*)

Silence

Part Four

The glory of the Lord shall be revealed: and all humankind shall see it.
(Isaiah 40:5)

Readings

Isaiah 40:1-5
Luke 1:26-38 – 'You are to conceive in your womb and bear a son, and you
must name him Jesus'
or Matthew 1:18-23
Revelation 21:1-7 – '. . . a new heaven and a new earth . . .'

Meditation: Mary, Mother of Jesus

I am old now, yet the memory of that incredible day when my son was
born is still carved upon my mind in clear, sculpted lines.

It was the beginning of an experience which has given me wondrous, indescribable joy, as well as indescribable pain.

Surely Simeon was right that day in the Temple, when he took my baby,
Jesus, in his arms and said to me that my baby, my beautiful boy, would be
misunderstood and contradicted and be the cause of the pain of a sword-
thrust through me.

And so it has been.

Joy and grief were woven together into a seamless whole as I watched my
wonderful boy grow into an even more wonderful man, full of grace and
truth and wisdom.

So strong, yet so tender and gentle.

Seemingly unafraid of anything, yet so quickly understanding and soothing
others' fears.

I feared.

I *feared* for *him*.

For his safety.

For his wellbeing.

Sometimes, I didn't understand what it was he had to do and then I feared
for his sanity.

And then, when they tortured him and put him to death, I thought I'd go out of my mind with grief.

The son whom I had brought into the world, nurtured and cared for, now hanging, twisted and bleeding and terribly abused, in so *much* agony.

And yet, at that time, he could still think of my needs and wellbeing, putting me into John's loving care.

Then – the utter, *blinding* joy of his resurrection!!

Each year, as his birthday draws near, the memories are *particularly* vivid . . .

Angels and shepherds, cattle and kings, sheep and a manger.

My beloved Joseph at my side – and my baby, Jesus, in my arms.

I would have had it all no other way.

To be chosen to be the mother of the Messiah, the Saviour of the World!

I am so blessed among women, that God should choose me, his humble handmaiden, for *so great* a privilege.

Thank you, God!

Hymn

'My song is love unknown' (346, *Hymns Old and New*)

Silence

Prayers and Blessing

Final hymn

'Tell out, my soul' (467, *Hymns Old and New*)

An after-dark Advent/Christmas Service for teenagers

Requirements

- Strobe light. This can be borrowed from a local DJ/club, etc., or bought. An adequate strobe light can be purchased quite cheaply.

- Music: ethereal-sounding: e.g. *Aspirant Sunset* CD by Rick Wakeman, President Records; or *Calm* double CD, BMG Telstar TV. Both of these are excellent purchases, which can be used in a wide variety of situations. Also: *Thankful* CD by MaryMary Columbia/CD2 Records, or – alternative, suggested by a consultant teenager (a very good idea to have one of these, if possible!) – *Black Nativity*: recording of the hit musical/similar music.

- Candles/nightlights sunk into containers of sand. Matches.

- Separate trays of sand in which to write names of those people/situations for whom people wish to pray.

- Diamonds/triangles/various shaped pieces of paper for other prayers, preferably multi-coloured.

- Pens.

- Small basket or bowl in front of the crib in which to place prayers.

- Also, mound/other shape, made of e.g. plasticine/sand, in which to 'plant' the prayer papers, if this is preferred.

- Cocktail sticks for the 'mound prayers'.

Note

- This service could be particularly effective if it is led, and the parts taken – particularly that of Jess – by older teenagers, who are confident in their ability to hold it all together.

- As with music, vogue words amongst teenagers are time-sensitive – and, sometimes, region-sensitive, as well. Try to find out – another use for your consultant teenager/s – what words are currently popular in your particular area.

Before the service

As people enter, the church is in darkness. The swirling strobe light, set to slow speed, is the only source of light. Meditative music is playing: e.g. *Aspirant Sunset*, or one of the tunes from *Calm*.

The service

Reader 1 (Unseen. From one side of the church)

The people who walked in darkness have seen a great light.

For those who lived in a land of deep shadows – light!

Sunbursts of light!

(Lights switched on throughout church/strobe off, during final sentence)

Reader 2 *(Unseen. From opposite side of the church)*

For a child has been born – for us!

The gift of a son – for us!

He'll take over the running of the world.

His names will be: Amazing Counsellor, Strong God, Eternal Father, Prince of Wholeness and Peace.

Song/Carol 1

Either 'Shackles' from CD *Thankful* (you could use the CD to accompany the singing) or 'Once in royal David's city' (preferably accompanied by music group, rather than organ).

JESS enters *carrying a large notebook and a pencil. Goes to front of church.*

Hi! My name is Jess.

I'm a cub reporter from *The Stone Tablets*.

My Editor has sent me to cover some truly weird events that appear to have been happening here, in Palestine.

There have been many accounts, some apparently confirmed by independent witnesses, of god-princes born in stables, bright stars, kings from far distant countries, shepherds leaving their flocks and rushing into town to see this stable-king . . .

Mad, huh?

My hunch is that the stories have all got hyped up, as they've gone from mouth to mouth.

I've a sinking feeling I've been dumped with a non-story that I'll have to make something of, in order to justify being sent here and to satisfy my Editor – else my job will be on the line.

Huh! Joke. Get it? Journalist? On the line?

Oh, never mind. Forget it.

Still, I've never been to this area before, so my plan is to cobble together a few interviews and reflections – that shouldn't take *too* long – then I'll take some time out and do a bit of exploring, on expenses. My Editor need never know.

I've been doing a bit of background research just, you know, to pad out the article and give it a bit more depth than it's likely to have, otherwise.

Apparently, there have been prophesies of the birth of a Messiah, who is to be the Saviour of the world, for *hundreds* of years in the Jewish scriptures. That one you heard earlier, that's from Isaiah and he's supposed to be top-prophet in this regard.

I'm actually about to speak with this god-prince's mum and her hubby.

I arranged to meet them here. I hope they're going to turn up . . .

Ah! Here they are.

***Enter MARY and JOSEPH**, who join Jess at the front.*

JESS How do you do. Thank you so much for agreeing to speak with me, Mr and Mrs – er . . .

MARY *(smiling)* Just call me Mary, Mother of Jesus.

JOSEPH And my name is Joseph. I am Mary's husband.

JESS Oh. Right. And I'm Jess.

Um. There have been many stories of some extraordinary happenings in Bethlehem and I gather that you are the best people to talk to.

Mary, Mother of Jesus, would you be so kind as to tell us how it all began?'

MARY I have lived in Nazareth – a town in the northern hills of Galilee, as I'm sure you know – all my life.

I have been betrothed to Joseph, who is a carpenter by trade, since I was a young girl.

One day, not long before we were to be married, as I sat quietly, sewing my trousseau, a strange brightness fell on the cloth I was stitching. Startled, I looked up.

A mighty angel of God was standing in the little room, filling it with his presence.

Not surprisingly, I was very shaken indeed to be visited by such a heavenly being.

But he reassured me. 'Don't be frightened, Mary,' he said. 'My name is Gabriel, and I have been sent by God. You have nothing to fear. God has a surprise for you.'

'*Me?*' I exclaimed.

'Yes, you,' he said, gently. 'Do you think that God only deals with what the world thinks of as "the important people"? You are to bear a son. His name will be Jesus, because that means "the one who saves". God's power will rest on you and his Holy Spirit will come to you. Jesus will be very special. He will be called the Son of God and he will be the long-awaited King, whose kingdom will last for ever.'

'I'm not sure I understand,' I said, quietly. 'But I'm the Lord's maidservant, ready to serve, and to do anything he asks of me. Let it be with me just as you say.'

With that, the Angel Gabriel disappeared.

JOSEPH Some time after this, the edict from Emperor Augustus of Rome, that he wished to know just how many subjects he had and how much tax he could hope to collect from them, was issued. As you know, he ordered a numbering, or census, of everyone in his empire.

To do this, as you also know, everyone had to return to his home town to register.

For us, it meant a journey of nearly a week, travelling south to my home town of Bethlehem. I walked and Mary rode on a donkey. The terrain was rough and we had to travel over a mountainous and desert route.

Mary was well advanced in her pregnancy and she was utterly exhausted by the time we reached our destination.

Bethlehem was *teeming* with people, all come for the census.

The bustle and noise was incredible.

We might have enjoyed it all in another situation, but not with Mary in her condition.

We searched everywhere for a room, but every one in every inn was taken.

We were in despair: Mary knew she was about to give birth.

At the final inn we visited, the innkeeper took pity on us and suggested the cave where his animals were kept.

As he said, it would be better than nothing.

JESS   We'll hold the story at that point for a few moments, if you agree, in order to take in what you have told us. It truly is incredible.

Carol 2

'Silent Night' (444, *Hymns Old and New*)

*During the carol, **Mary and Joseph move aside**, down the side aisle. When the carol has finished, **some shepherds (S1, S2 and S3) enter** noisily down the centre aisle. They are laughing and joking and good-naturedly pushing and shoving one another.*

JESS   We are joined now by some shepherds, who have an equally amazing experience to tell. Gentlemen, perhaps . . .

S1   Yeah! Too right we would!! Mind you, I don't expect you'd believe it necessarily, being one of them sin-i-kil newspaper johnnies. But whatever you think and write about it not being true won't take away from the actual truth of the matter.

It were like this, see.

We was in the fields just outside Bethlehem, minding the sheep and our own business.

It were an ordinary night, like any other night. Some of us was posted to keep a lookout for wolves, slingshots at the ready, whilst others of us was telling stories to while away the time and keep ourselves awake.

I was just in the middle of this yarn when, *suddenly*, the quiet night sky was a *blaze* of light!

It was dazzling bright – yet not painful at all to look at, if you get my meaning.

S2 We looked up, and there were this glorious, *shining* figure of an angel, standing right there in front of us, as close to us as we is to you. *Huge*, he was.

We weren't half terrified!

But the angel says to us, real gentle like, 'Don't be frightened. I've come with the best news for you, which will bring you great joy. Not only for you, but for the *whole* world.

'Go into Bethlehem,' he said. 'And there you will find a baby, lying in a manger, wrapped in swaddling clothes. This baby is the Saviour of the world.'

'In a *manger*?' I says, disbelievin', like.

S3 At that moment, the *whole* sky came alive with angels, and the air was *filled* with their singing as they poured out a hymn of praise and thanksgiving to God. It was *A-MAZING*!

S1 Yeah! 'Glory to God in the highest,' they sang. 'And peace on earth to all people.'

It was *beautiful*!! I've never heard nothing like it. Nor never will again, neither, I don't suppose. Though, after all of that, I'd believe *any*thing could happen.

I wonder why they picked on *us* to tell. I mean, shepherds ain't exactly pukka people, are they. But, whatever the reason, I'm surely glad they did. I wouldn't have missed what we saw, not for a *world* of wealth and privilege.

S2 Nah. Me neither!

S3 Nor me!

*As they finish talking, **three regal-looking wise men enter** down the centre aisle, and the **shepherds step aside** respectfully, as the new arrivals join the group at the front.*

JESS *Thank* you, Your Highnesses, for agreeing to join me for this interview. I'm *most* grateful. Could I prevail upon you to tell us why you are here, in Bethlehem; so far from your homeland?

KING 1 *(inclining his head regally)* Of course. We would be delighted.

Well, it is not only the people of Israel who have been looking for a great king, promised by God.

Tales of this God-King have spread far and wide, over the centuries. Wise and learned men in lands near and far have waited for One who is to be born in the land of the Jews and who will rule the world in justice and peace.

Something, I am sure you will agree, we *all* yearn for.

My companions and I, we are astrologers, learned in the ways of the stars and the movements of the firmament. For years we have studied in various areas of learning – but there is always yet more to discover. Such is the wonder of wisdom.

KING 2 Then, one night, we noticed a star in the sky that was shining with a special brightness. We checked our charts, but could not identify it. It seemed to have appeared suddenly, mysteriously.

Such a star, we knew, must be the sign that a great king had been born! Could it, we wondered, *possibly* be the One for whom the world has been waiting and longing . . .

KING 3 So we set off, with rich gifts suitable to give to a king.

We have followed the bright star on a journey that has taken us many months. We have known the searing heat of the desert and the bone-chilling cold of the mountain. Travelled through Persia and Babylon and the wastes of Syria. Crossed mighty rivers . . .

KING 1 Until, at last, the star stopped over a small town.

Could this *really* be our journey's end, we wondered, for the star was shining down, not on a palace, but a cave set in the hillside, used for housing animals.

Was this *really* the place where the Saviour of the world had been born, and whom we had travelled so far to worship?

JESS Thank you, Your Highnesses. With your permission, I think we'll pause for a few moments to reflect on all you and the shepherds have told us, before we turn once more to speak to Jesus' mother.

Meditative music

Suggestion: either 'Sweet little Jesus boy, we made you be born in a manger' sung by Princess Stewart, from the *Black Nativity* recording, or one of the tracks from *Calm*.

*During this, the **Kings step back and Mary steps forward** to join Jess.*

JESS Mary, Mother of Jesus, would you care to continue this incredible story.

MARY Well, the cave to which the innkeeper had directed us was, not surprisingly, a dirty and smelly place.

Animal droppings covered the floor.

But it was warm. And it was private.

I had been so frightened, at one point, that I would have to give birth in the street.

Joseph quickly made a bed of straw for me, from a clean supply he found in a rack on the wall, and then he cleaned up the stable as best he could.

By now my pains were very strong and frequent.

In between tending and trying to help me, he laid some fresh straw in the manger for a crib.

Then, there, in the dimness and among the animals, my wondrous, my *beautiful* baby was born.

I wrapped him in swaddling bands, fed him, then laid him to sleep in the manger.

Carol 3

'Be still, for the presence of the Lord' (53, *Hymns Old and New*)

During this, **Mary steps back, and shepherds and kings step forward**.

JESS	*(addressing the shepherds)* So, gentlemen, we left you listening to the angels. What happened next?
S2	As suddenly as the sky had been filled with light and music, it all became quiet and dark.

We kept asking one another: 'Did *you* see and hear what *I* saw and heard?'

It were as if we couldn't believe such a wonderful thing could or would have happened to such ordinary folk as us.

But, no. It *hadn't* been a dream.

So we drew straws and left the unlucky one who had drawn the short straw guarding the sheep, whilst the rest of us set out, at a run, for the nearby town of Bethlehem.

S3	Somehow, although we had no idea where, precisely, we were to go, we went straight to the right place. It were as if our feet was guided independently of us.

It were a night packed *full* of miracles.

S1	And there, lying in a manger, just as we had been told, was a new-born babe.

We knelt and worshipped him.

Then we gave our gift of the best lamb from our flocks.

JESS	*(turning to the kings)* And you, Your Highnesses?
K3	We went into the stable.

Then we, who are used to people bowing the knee to us, we knelt in the dust and dirt of the stable – and were honoured to do so.

We felt humbled in the presence of The Holy One.

Tiny babe though he was, there was a heavenly aura about him which radiated outwards and enfolded everyone in its loving embrace.

We, too, had gifts to give to the Saviour of the world.

Mine was myrrh. The precious and fragrant spice used in burying the dead. A sign of the sorrow I instinctively felt was to come for him.

K2   My gift was frankincense. The sweet-smelling and pure incense offered in worship in the temples of our land. It is only used in the most holy of situations, and it is forbidden for it to be used for any other purpose than to be offered in worship.

K1   And I gave gold, the colour of the sun. A gift fit for a king.

JESS   Mary, Mother of Jesus, Joseph, gentlemen, Your Highnesses – *thank you*. *(He bows his head graciously to each, as he says their name)*

Carol 4

'See him lying on a bed of straw' (440, *Hymns Old and New*)

JESS   Well, as you know, I *began* this report full of cynicism and disbelief.

That shepherd – wise man that *he* was – he saw right through me, didn't he, when he spoke of me as 'one of those cynical newspaper johnnies'!

But, what I have heard and seen has *totally* turned me around.

There is *no* doubting the conviction of the stories we have been told today.

You *know* the truth, when you hear it. It has a resonance that is unmistakable.

Before I arrived, I had penned my article in my mind: the seemingly innocent introduction, some first-hand accounts, then a few tongue-in-cheek comments, followed by a cynical and dismissive conclusion.

Now, I have thrown all that away and I shall begin again, from the beginning.

What I shall write will melt the hearts of the readers of *The Stone Tablets*.

I shall witness to all I have seen and heard.

God has given me a new heart and put a new spirit in me.

He has removed from me my heart of stone and given me a heart of flesh, in its place.

I have been reborn with the Baby of Bethlehem!

It's heavy, man! Sound! *(Jess punches the air exuberantly)*

Thanks be to God!

Jess exits, *whooping and dancing*.

Song

Suggestion: 'Be happy' sung by MaryMary on their CD *Thankful*. (Chorus: My heart has found a new beat ever since you came into my life . . .)
(Invite the congregation to clap and sing along – have the words printed or, preferably, up on an OHP – and to dance in the aisles)

Prayers

- Reduce lighting as much as possible, only leaving sufficient on so that people can see to write their prayers, etc.

- Leader of prayers invites anyone who wishes, to come up and light a candle/nightlight for a person or situation that they wish to hold before God.

  Also invite them to write the name of the situation/person in one of the trays of sand; or on one of the flags and place it in the small basket in front of the crib, or attach to a cocktail stick and put on the mound.

  Play a track/s from *Aspirant Sunset* or *Calm* whilst all this is being done.

- When the above has been completed, all other lights off, so that the only light is the flickering of the lit candles.

- Now candles can be lit on behalf of everyone present for, for example, the homeless; the lonely; those unable to celebrate Christmas, or their Christian faith, freely. Say a short prayer as each candle is lit, and follow this with a moment or two of silence.

- Other prayers, as required.

- If possible, beforehand ask two or three of those who will be at the Service to write and read the prayers that are on behalf of the congregation.

Blessing

Final carol

'Hark, the herald-angels sing' (199, *Hymns Old and New*)

Follow with hot mince pies, hot coffee and chilled cola.

Christmas Eve/Christmas Day Children's Service

Before the service

- As children enter, have Box of delights (see Resources section) ready and give each child a musical instrument, windsock banner or dancing ribbons and a head/wrist/ankle band of tinsel.

- Have some children already dressed up as characters from the Nativity story.

- Either they, or other children, can carry their character or another figure or item from the crib scene.

- Everyone enters to lively music, e.g. a medley of children's carols, preferably played on a piano, guitar, electric keyboard, or on a CD.

The service

Leader

Welcome. Introduction and explanation about the Service.

A procession of the children

. . . who are dressed up/carrying the crib scene figures, enters.

As the procession comes down the church, **everyone is invited to join** on the end.

The procession weaves in and out of the aisles, with everyone blowing, banging or shaking their instrument, or waving their banner or dancing ribbons and finally arrives at the crib scene.

Instruments and banners, etc., laid down and all the children gather round and sit down on the floor/cushions/kneelers/blankets. Parents go back to their places.

Narrator

At the appropriate points in the following, the Narrator pauses, in order to give the particular child time to place their figure/item in the crib scene.

Once, long ago, there was a young girl called Mary.

She lived in a small town called Nazareth.

One day as she sat in her room sewing, an angel appeared in front of her.

'Mary,' the angel said, 'God has chosen you to do something very important. You are going to have a very, *very* special baby. And you are to call him "Jesus".'

As you may imagine, Mary was *very* surprised *indeed* to be told this. But she loved God and she trusted him.

So she obediently accepted what the angel told her.

Some time later, when Mary was very pregnant, she and Joseph, her husband, had to travel from where they lived in Nazareth, to Bethlehem.

It was a *very* long journey and Mary was *ever* so tired when they finally arrived in Bethlehem.

The town was full to bursting point, with people rushing about busily.

No one had any time for Mary and Joseph, and their needs.

Mary and Joseph went *all* over Bethlehem, *desperately* searching for somewhere to stay.

But *everywhere* was full:

'Sorry. No room *here*.'

'Nope. We're full right up.'

'A *room*? You must be joking!'

Mary knew she was about to give birth.

She and Joseph were in despair.

'Please, *please* help us!' Joseph begged at the last inn. 'You are our final hope. We have tried everywhere and there is no room in any of the boarding places.

'My wife is about to have a baby. *Please, don't* turn us away.'

'Well. There is the stable,' said the innkeeper, doubtfully. 'The animals are there, of course, so it's a bit *smelly*. But at least you'll be warm and dry.'

'Yes. Yes!' said Joseph, eagerly. '*Thank you*! Oh, thank you. We'll take it!'

The innkeeper led them to the stable and Joseph quickly set about spreading some clean straw on the floor for Mary to lie on.

Then he put some more clean straw in the manger, to act as a crib for the new baby.

The animals did not seem at all surprised to have to share their stable in this way and just carried on munching.

There, in the dimness, amidst the animal smells and noise, Mary's baby was born.

Joseph and Mary gazed in wonder at him.

He was so *beautiful*.

From the top of his head, to the tip of his tiny toes.

Their hearts were brimming over with love and joy.

Then Mary wrapped him up in long strips of cloth, called swaddling bands – as mothers did in those days – and laid him in the manger.

'The angel said we were to call him "Jesus",' Mary said softly, as she gently stroked his cheek with her finger.

Joseph nodded. 'Yes. "Jesus" means "The One who Saves". A perfect name for the Saviour of the world.'

Carol

'Away in a manger' (modern version) (51, *Hymns Old and New*). The children who are too young to sing can play their instruments or wave their streamers or banners.

Narrator

There were shepherds in the fields around Bethlehem, guarding their flocks of sheep.

They warmed themselves by the fire and told stories to while away the time.

Suddenly, the night sky was *ablaze* with light! And there, standing before them, was an angel.

The shepherds were *terrified* – 'Well, you don't see angels *every* day, do you,' one of them said later.

'Don't be afraid,' said the angel, smiling. 'I have some wonderful news for you.

'Today, in Bethlehem, a *very* special baby was born. He is the Saviour of the world.

'At this very moment, he is lying in a manger in a stable.

'Go and see him for yourselves and worship him, as he deserves.'

Then, the whole sky *filled* with angels *singing* and *praising* God.

Then, as suddenly as they had come, the angels disappeared.

The shepherds looked at one another, rubbing their eyes.

'Did *you* see what *I* saw?' they asked one another.

They all nodded.

It had *really* happened.

'*Hey!* What are we waiting for? Let's go, then!' they said.

Whooping and singing with excitement, they rushed across the fields and into town.

When they found Mary and Joseph, and the baby lying in a manger, they fell on their knees before him.

Tears of wonder ran down their faces.

Then they pushed forward the youngest, a shepherd boy.

He was carrying a newborn lamb, which he shyly laid in front of the manger.

Carol

'Infant Holy, Infant Lowly' or 'While shepherds watched'
(251 or 554, *Hymns Old and New*)
(*Instruments and banners, etc., as before*)

Narrator

Meanwhile, some wise men had been following a bright star in the sky.

They believed it was a special sign that a great king had been born.

The wise men had been journeying for a *long* time, from a far-off country.

Now they rode into the little town of Bethlehem.

At last they had reached their destination.

As you may imagine, they caused quite a stir with their fine clothes and many camels.

To the wise men's surprise, the bright star stopped – not over a palace where they would expect to find a king but over a simple little dwelling cut out of the hillside.

But the wise men were also men of great faith.

They did not doubt that God had led them to the right place.

As they entered they saw Mary with the baby Jesus.

The three wise men knelt on the dusty floor in their fine clothes, and bowed low before the baby Jesus in worship.

They knew that this tiny baby would grow up to be far, *far* greater than they, or *anyone* else in the world, had *ever* been.

Then they gave Jesus their gifts.

Gold: a gift fit for a king.

Frankincense: the sweet-smelling incense used in worship in the temples of their homeland.

Myrrh: a fragrant spice which was used for perfuming the bodies of people who had died. Myrrh was a symbol of sorrow and sadness.

Mary thought that the last gift was bit strange for a baby.

But the wise men knew that the Scriptures said that the Christ-child would take the sorrows and cares of the whole world on his own shoulders when he grew up.

Giving myrrh was a way of showing they knew that this baby was the One who had been promised by God.

Jesus was the One whom the world had been waiting for, for such a very long time.

When the wise men had left, Mary gave Jesus a feed and tucked him down to sleep.

Carol

'Little Jesus, sweetly sleep' (306, *Hymns Old and New*)
(Instruments, banners, streamers, as before)

Leader

Give time for answers for each of the following questions:

- My memory is not what it was. You'll have to remind me. What did the shepherds and the wise men give Jesus?

- Do you think the shepherds and the wise men gave Jesus anything else?

- What would *you* want to bring to give to Baby Jesus?

- What do *you* think was the most special gift for Jesus?

- Do you know what *I* think was the most special gift, so far as Jesus was concerned?

  The people themselves: the shepherds and the wise men.

  They came themselves, in person.

  The shepherds left their sheep – their livelihood.

  The wise men travelled for a long time and a great distance. They didn't send a servant and stay comfortably at home themselves.

  By each of them coming themselves, *in person*, they showed their love for Jesus.

  And it is the same for *all* of us.

  For *me* . . .

  For *you* . . .

  And *you* . . .

  And *you* . . .
  (Point right round the circle, as you say the above)

- The most special gift of all that we can give Jesus, is OURSELVES.

  Remind me: *What is the* most special gift we can give Jesus?

  Pardon? I didn't quite get that. My hearing isn't what it was. Louder, please. *Much* louder!

  Oh, yes. Thank you. Much better. I think I heard it all right that time!

Carol

'See him lying on a bed of straw' (vv 1-4 and chorus) (440, *Hymns Old and New*)

Leader

Now, our prayers:

Baby Jesus,
   we love you.
Thank you
   for being born
   for us.
Amen.

Gentle Jesus,
  help us to be
  loving and kind.
Just like you.
Amen.

Loving Jesus,
  wrap us,
  and our families
  and friends,
  in your love
  and care,
  this Christmas
  and always.
Amen.

Kind Jesus,
  we pray for all those
  who are sad and lonely,
  especially
  at this happy time.
Stay close by them.
Hold them tight,
  so that the strength
  and warmth
  of your love
  will melt their sadness
  and loneliness
  all away.
Amen.

Now, our Blessing:

May the love of the Baby Jesus
  surround you.
May the joy of the Baby Jesus
  be heard in your laughter and joy.
May the peace of the Baby Jesus
  fill your hearts and your lives
  this Christmas
  and always.
Amen.

Three cheers for Baby Jesus!
(Encourage everyone to clap, cheer, bang their instruments, wave their banners
and streamers, etc. – in fact, to make an exuberant noise)

Final carol

'Heaven invites you to a party' (last three verses) (150, The Source)

The children lead a final procession round the church, *to as much celebration as possible.*

Have a bowl of sweets held ready by the exit so that each child is given one as they leave.

Christingle Service

Christingle is a well known and much loved form of service.

The service offered here can be used in its entirety, or as a base upon which to plan your own particular service.

As Christingle is a service of light, light should be its central theme with regard to presentation.

Preparation

For the Talk

- As large a spherical object as possible, e.g. a red space-hopper, or a papier-mâché ball painted orange/red, or covered with orange/red crepe paper or material.
- A good quantity of Blu-Tack, spread thickly over the top of the space hopper/papier mache ball, in order to attach the sticks and holder for the candle.
- Four kebab sticks (or similar).
- A large, slim white candle and holder.
- Dried fruit or jelly baby sweets.
- Matches.

Also

- Box of delights: instruments, banners, windsocks, dancing ribbons (see Resources section).
- Sufficient numbers of prepared individual Christingles.
- Matches and tapers.
- Service sheets.

Music

If possible, use informal accompaniment, e.g, guitar, piano, drums electric violin or prerecorded music.

Suggest to the local primary school that they come and lead the singing or do a special spot, such as sing the Christingle song. (Ensure that the parents know they are very welcome as well.)

Before the service

Lively music when the children enter.

If possible, have some simple songs with actions, that can be led from the front, that everyone can do whilst they wait for the service to begin.

The service

Leader

Welcome.

Introduction and explanation about the service:

- That it will begin with a procession with all the children taking part.

- Explain about the instruments and how they can be used, if any are unusual.

- Also demonstrate how to swirl the dancing streamers.

- Invite the children out and give each one either an instrument or a wind-sock/banner or dancing streamer.

Procession

Candle-bearers lead the procession, weaving round the church to lively music, accompanied by the children playing their instruments, waving their banners, swirling their dancing streamers, etc.

Procession returns to the front, the instruments, banners, streamers, etc., are returned and the children go back to their places.

Leader

Q. 'What beautiful thing do you often see in the sky after it has rained?'

(**A.** Rainbow.)

Leader

A long, long time ago, *long* before the birth of Jesus, God made a promise.

He wanted to show everyone how *very* much he loved them. And he wanted to give a sign, so that every time people saw it, they would be reminded of God's love and commitment.

'I am going to make a promise,' God said. 'For as long as the earth lasts, I will send you day, and night, and the seasons of the year: a season for planting seeds – and, when those seeds have grown, a season for harvesting.

'I am going to give you a sign to remind you always of my promise.

'Whenever you look up into the sky, and see a rainbow, you will be reminded of what I have said.' (Genesis 9:13-15a)

The rainbow-coloured ribbons on the banners and streamers that some of you were carrying just now, remind us of that.

Then, many, *many* years later, God sent Jesus to remind us of *another* promise God had made.

This promise was that he would send his Son, Jesus, to show all of us the way back to God.

And so, on the very first Christmas Day the Baby Jesus, the Saviour of the world, was born.

Jesus, the Light of the World!

Carol

'See him lying on a bed of straw' (440, *Hymns Old and New*)

Talk

(Have the artefacts listed at the beginning nearby, but out of sight.)

Ask if the children have ever heard the story of *James and the Giant Peach*. (Roald Dahl is still very popular with young children.)

Then say, well, you may not have the largest peach in the world, but you *do* have the largest orange. (Bring it out of its hiding place.)

Say that you also have some other items (bring them out, on a tray): a ribbon, some sticks with fruit, etc., on, and a candle.

Then look very worried and scratch your head.

Tell them you're a lot older now and that your memory is not what it used to be. It's an awful long time since last Christmas and you are going to need the children to help you remember what all these things mean and how to put them all together.

Then get the children to tell you and help you.

If appropriate, ask for volunteers to come out and help you construct the Christingle.

An alternative

Do the above, but give incorrect meanings to the symbolisms.

However, this only works if you are certain that there are children in the congregation who know the true meanings *and* who are prepared to correct you.

Reminder: The orange = the world; the red ribbon = Jesus' sacrifice on the cross; the four sticks = the seasons; the fruit on the sticks = the fruits of the earth; and the candle = the light of Christ.

When the Christingle is constructed, thank the children and say how important they have been.

Now you remember it all, perfectly.

Recap on the meaning and symbolism and add in anything else you wish to say. But keep it tight. Less is always more, with children.

The Christingle song

'Can you see what we have made for this very special day?' (65, *The Source*)

Leader

Just as you have come to worship and to celebrate the birth of Jesus, the Light of the World, today, 2000 years ago shepherds and kings came to worship and to celebrate the birth of God's Light.

The shepherds were summoned by angels.

And the three wise men were led by a bright, shining star.

The shepherds gave a lamb.

And the three wise men gave gold, frankincense and myrrh.

Now it is your turn to offer your gifts.

Some of you have brought your gifts in Christingle envelopes.

But don't worry if you haven't, you can put your offering onto the collection plate.

In a moment, I'm going to invite all the children to come up and give their gifts. Then you will be able to collect your very own Christingle – not as big as the one we made earlier, though!

When you have collected your Christingle everyone is going to form a chain round the church so that, when the Christingles are lit, the church will be circled with light.

('We three kings of Orient are' can be played as background music, as the children come up with their gifts and to collect their Christingles.)

(When everyone is in place, the Christingles are lit.)

Prayers

Remind everyone that they can join themselves to each prayer in a very special way by saying 'Amen', which means 'So be it', or 'I agree, may it happen'.

Jesus,
   Light of the World,
   shine in my heart,
   shine in my life,
   now and always,
   so that I may be a light for others.
Amen.

Jesus,
   we pray for all the children,
   everywhere,
   who are ill,
   or sad,
   or lonely,
   or scared,
   today.
May the warmth
   and the light
   of your love
   wrap closely round them,
   like swaddling cloths,
   and keep them safe.

May it melt
   all their dark clouds
   away.
Amen.

Jesus,
   thank you for our special people.
Take care of them
   and bless them.
Help us to be
   Christingle children
   to them.
Amen.

Leader

Now, we are going to blow out the candles on each of our Christingles. But the light has not gone out, for it continues to shine in our hearts and our lives.

All together, now!

BLOW!

(Children return to their seats, taking their Christingles with them.)

Hymn

'Colours of day dawn into the mind' (87, *Hymns Old and New*/69, *The Source*)

Leader

We are nearly at the end of our service.

Now remind me again – what do the different parts of the Christingle stand for?

(Allow time for the children to respond.)

Blessing

May the Baby Jesus
   be born in your hearts.
May the Light of Jesus
   light your way.
May the love of God the Father,
   his Son, Jesus
   and the Holy Spirit,
   surround you
   and keep you safe,
   today,
   tomorrow
   and always.
Amen.

Final hymn

'One more step along the world I go' (405, *Hymns Old and New*)

Invite the children to come up and collect an instrument, banner, etc., and to process round the church, either during the hymn, or after as a finale.

Resources section

Box of delights

When my children were small, we had an 'Ever-so-useful box'.

This contained a huge variety of potentially useful bits and pieces, that could be used in making models/fancy dress costumes/resources for endless imaginary games.

Into this box would go such things as empty cereal boxes, bright tissue or wrapping paper, aluminium foil, glue, scissors, felt, colouring pencils and paints, old cards, loo roll and kitchen towel cardboard inners, lengths and bits of material.

You name it, it could usually be found in the 'Ever-so-useful box'.

For years after my children grew beyond the stage of needing such a resource, I would have to force myself to throw away anything that I would formerly have put in the ESUB.

The Box of delights has a similar function to the ESU box.

Over the months leading up to Christmas, get church members to collect any bits and pieces that could be used for making the following:

Home-made instruments

- Place the same sized pebbles in tins and bind the lids shut very securely with masking tape. Place different sizes in different tins to make a variety of sound when shaken.

- The time-honoured tissue paper over a comb.

- Bicycle bell or old-fashioned car horn.

- Metal discs of varying sizes with a hole punched in the middle, strung onto a string, and shaken.

- Stiff brush rubbed over a rough surface.

- Two pieces of wood or hollow cane, banged together.

The above are just some examples of what can be contrived out of very simple equipment. Virtually anything can be pressed into service.

These make a good addition to conventional instruments, which can usually be borrowed from local schools for use in special services.

Windsock banners

Equipment needed

- Pieces of hollow garden cane, of varying lengths to suit the different sizes of children who will be carrying them.

- Wire that is pliable enough to bend into a circle, yet strong enough to retain its shape.

- Lengths of a variety of different, brightly coloured ribbon, preferably 2.5-5 cm wide.

Cut the cane to the appropriate lengths.

Cut the ribbons into lengths about 5 cm longer than these.

Cut the wire into pieces long enough to bend into circles with a diameter of 15-20 cm, and leaving extra at each end easily long enough to push into one end of the hollow cane. Ensure that the wire is firmly fixed inside the cane.

Bend the circle of wire, so that it is at 90 degrees to the piece of cane.

Attach appropriate lengths of each coloured ribbon to each wire: the ribbons should be almost as long as the cane. Continue around the wire circle, until it is covered with ribbons.

Dancing streamers

Equipment needed

- Short pieces of stick, approximately 30-40 cm long.

- Wide ribbon, with as much body and substance to it as possible, in a variety of bright colours.

Cut these ribbons to the appropriate lengths for children of different ages and attach to the sticks.

When waved or swirled, e.g. in circles or figures of eight, these ribbons can be made to 'dance'.

Head/arm/wrist/ankle bands

These are simply pieces of tinsel, cut into varying lengths and put round a child's head, arm, wrist or ankle – whichever they choose.

Suggestion

Why not have a Workshop, during the autumn half-term, or one weekend, when children can help to make the above.

Christmas Quiz and Wordsearch

Answer the quiz, then find the answers in the wordsearch

1. Who is Christmas all about?

2. In which month was he born?

3. Was he born in a: a) Palace. b) Semi-detached? c) Stable? d) Hotel?

4. In which town did this happen?

5. What was the name of his mother?

6. What was the name of her husband?

7. Who did angels appear to, to announce Jesus' birth?

8. Who else came to visit Jesus?

9. What did they follow to find where Jesus was?

10. What gifts did they bring?

11. What was the name of the king who told them to 'go and find where this child is, then bring me the news so I can go and worship him'?

12. Were the king's intentions good or evil?

13. In which town did Mary receive a visit from an angel, telling her she was to be the mother of the Saviour of the World?

14. What was the reason for Mary and Joseph's journey to Bethlehem? Was it: a) Shopping? b) Holiday? c) Census? d) They were bored?

15. In what did Mary lay her baby when he was born?

16. What does the name 'Jesus' mean?

17. Who told them to use the stable?

18. Eight days after Jesus' birth, Mary and Joseph took him where?

19. Who did they meet there?

20. What are the four weeks leading up to Christmas called?

```
J   E   S   U   S   D   P   Z   A   D   S
B   O   X   Y   K   K   I   N   G   E   A
N   E   Y   S   T   A   B   L   E   C   V
O   H   T   E   R   A   Z   A   N   E   I
F   L   B   H   C   N   X   Q   U   M   O
G   O   D   L   L   O   V   E   H   B   U
P   W   L   I   V   E   M   S   R   E   R
N   E   D   A   D   M   H   F   R   R   E
E   D   A   R   O   I   Q   E   Y   T   S
M   Z   A   C   R   S   P   L   M   W   N
E   T   X   Z   E   O   Y   B   V   E   E
S   D   R   E   H   P   E   H   S   N   C
I   W   Y   R   O   L   G   F   Q   T   N
W   A   L   J   J   K   M   A   R   Y   I
E   S   O   D   G   O   L   D   Z   F   K
E   A   R   V   D   U   S   Q   C   I   N
R   E   D   M   Q   L   T   E   D   F   A
H   L   D   V   A   K   I   X   P   T   R
T   P   Z   C   E   N   M   N   V   H   F
H   M   A   V   E   N   G   T   G   B   A
C   E   N   S   U   S   T   E   A   M   N
R   T   Y   I   N   N   I   N   R   Q   G
R   E   P   E   E   K   D   O   W   Z   E
S   Y   C   M   E   S   S   I   A   H   L
```

There are also 11 further words and 1 phrase hidden in the wordsearch.

They are: LOVE, JOY, PEACE, MESSIAH, HOPE, KING, LORD, ANGEL, LIVE, GLORY, YES, SON OF GOD.

Can you find them?